Literacy Consultants
DAVID BOOTH • KATHLEEN GOULD LUNDY

Social Studies Consultant
PETER PAPPAS

A Harcourt Achieve Imprint

10801 N. Mopac Expressway
Building # 3
Austin, TX 78759
1.800.531.5015

Steck-Vaughn is a trademark of Harcourt Achieve Inc. registered in the United States of America and/or other jurisdictions. All inquiries should be mailed to: Paralegal Department, 6277 Sea Harbor Drive, Orlando, FL 32887.

Ru*bicon © 2007 Rubicon Publishing Inc.
www. rubiconpublishing.com

Project Editor: Kim Koh
Editor: Vicki Low
Art Director: Jen Harvey
Project Designer: Jan-John Rivera

7 8 9 10 11   5 4 3 2 1

Marco Polo and the Roc
ISBN 13: 978-1-4190-3203-5
ISBN 10:   1-4190-3203-8

Printed in Singapore

PHOTO CREDITS: istockphoto: 2-5, 13, 21, 29, 37, 45-47; indexopen: 13, 46-47; The Granger Collection, New York: 4, 21, 29, 37, 45-46

MARCO POLO AND THE ROC

Written by

DAVID BOYD

Illustrated by

DREW NG

MARCO POLO

KUBLAI KHAN

RUSTI

TING LING

REAL PEOPLE IN HISTORY

MARCO POLO (1254–1324): Brave and adventurous, he was known for his travels throughout Europe and Asia.

KUBLAI KHAN (1215–1294): A powerful and fierce warrior, he was also known as the Great Khan.

RUSTICHELLO (RUSTI): He was in the same prison as Marco Polo. He listened to Marco's stories and wrote them down.

FICTIONAL CHARACTER

TING LING: The interpreter in the court of Kublai Khan, she sailed with Marco Polo to search for the Roc.

Contents

4 Introduction

6 Chapter 1: Captured!
13 **Time Out:** Venice

14 Chapter 2: The Great Khan
21 **Time Out:** Kublai Khan

22 Chapter 3: On the High Seas
29 **Time Out:** Chinese Junks

30 Chapter 4: The Roc
37 **Time Out:** The Legend of the Roc

38 Chapter 5: Celebration!
45 **Time Out:** The Capital City

46 Moving On: Did Marco Make It All Up?

Marco Polo was one of the greatest travelers of his time. He traveled from Venice in Europe to Asia, and he visited China during the reign of the great Kublai Khan.

Marco Polo was impressed with the things he saw in China, such as paper currency, coal, and the imperial postal system. He became a good friend of Kublai Khan and stayed in China for 17 years. When he returned to Venice, Marco Polo published a book about his travels. The book amazed its readers and became very popular. It made him famous.

Marco Polo

TIMELINE

1254	1260	1271	1275	1292
Marco Polo is born in Venice, Italy.	Kublai Khan, also called the Great Khan, establishes his court at Cambaluc.	Marco Polo sets out on his travels at the age of 17.	Marco Polo arrives in Cambaluc and sees many new things that impress him.	Marco Polo leaves China by sea for Persia. He escorts a Mongol princess on her way to marry the Persian king.

Europe and Asia in the 1300s

Atlantic Ocean

MONGOL EMPIRE

Indian Ocean

Kublai Khan and the Mongols were from Central Asia. They were nomads — people who moved from place to place and did not settle down in any one location. The Mongols were great horsemen who loved hunting. They were also mighty warriors. In Kublai Khan's time, the Mongols ruled over much of Europe, Asia, and the Middle East.

Kublai Khan was the first Mongol emperor of China. He set up his court in Cambaluc, now called Beijing. The Mongol rule in China is known as the Yuan dynasty.

Kublai Khan

WHAT'S THE STORY? This story is set in an actual time in history and depicts real people, but some of the characters and events are fictitious.

1294 »	1295 »	1298 »	1324 »	1368 »
Kublai Khan dies after a long and remarkable reign.	Marco Polo returns to Venice.	Marco Polo publishes a book about his travels and adventures.	Marco Polo dies at the age of 70.	The Mongols are driven out of China.

Chapter 1: Captured!

THE YEAR IS 1298. VENICE IS AT WAR.

THE RING OF STEEL AGAINST STEEL, THE CHEERS OF VICTORIOUS MEN, AND THE PAINFUL CRIES OF THE CONQUERED.

THE VENETIANS ARE DEFEATED. SOME ARE KILLED, OTHERS ARE BADLY WOUNDED, AND THE REST ARE CAPTURED.

VENICE

A city of canals

Venice ●
● Genoa
Pisa ●

ITALY

Venice, located on the northeast coast of Italy, was a trading seaport in Marco Polo's time. It was rich and powerful. Other seaports at that time were Genoa and Pisa.

For centuries, Venice could be reached only by boat. It was not until modern times that the city was linked with the rest of Italy by rail and road.

Venice is now part of Italy. It is known for its canals, gondolas, churches, and historic buildings. The city is built on 118 islands. In addition to its maze of streets, there are 180 canals and 400 bridges. What a unique city!

Gondola

Chapter 2: The Great Khan

THE GREAT KHAN WELCOMES MARCO TO HIS COURT. HE IS PLEASED WITH MARCO'S GOOD MANNERS.

HE MOTIONS TO A YOUNG WOMAN, WHO COMES FORWARD.

MY NAME IS TING LING. I WILL TRANSLATE FOR MY MASTER, THE GREAT KHAN.

THANK YOU. I'M MARCO POLO.

THE GREAT KHAN ASKS MANY QUESTIONS ABOUT VENICE AND LISTENS EAGERLY TO MARCO. TING LING TRANSLATES FOR OVER AN HOUR.

VERY QUICKLY, THEY PREPARE FOR THE JOURNEY.

A SHIP WITH A CREW OF 200 MEN IS READY TO TAKE MARCO AND TING LING TO SHANGHAI, THEN HONG KONG, AND THEN ON TO AFRICA AND THE ISLAND OF MADAGASCAR, JUST OFF THE COAST OF MOZAMBIQUE.

MARCO IS UNSURE OF WHAT TO EXPECT, BUT HE IS READY FOR HIS ADVENTURE. HE IS HAPPY THAT TING LING WILL BE WITH HIM.

I'M READY FOR WHATEVER COMES.

IT WILL BE ALL RIGHT, MARCO. THE GREAT KHAN CANNOT BE WRONG.

KUBLAI KHAN

Kublai Khan was a great Mongol leader. Under his rule, the Mongols conquered all of China. They established their capital city on the site of present-day Beijing.

Trade flourished during the reign of Kublai Khan. He welcomed foreigners to his court. Merchants came from Russia, the Middle East, and Europe. As a young man, Marco Polo visited the court of Kublai Khan in 1275.

Kublai Khan was the first ruler to introduce paper money in China. He also set up a postal system (described in this story), and a tax system that forced his people to give money to the emperor.

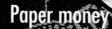

Paper money

Chinese junk

CHINESE JUNKS

I n Marco Polo's time, the Chinese sailed all over the world in huge ships made of teak (a very hard wood) and bamboo. These ships were called junks, and they were much larger than ships used by the Europeans. Marco Polo reported seeing ships that had 60 cabins on board and could house as many as 300 men!

The Chinese were way ahead of the West in the techniques and instruments they used in sailing. For instance, Chinese captains used magnetic compasses to sail their ships across the seas.

The Chinese were such expert sailors that some people today think they discovered America before Columbus did! What do you think?

Silk Road — trade route across Asia

Chapter 4: The Roc

"THEY ARE EGGS! BUT THEY'RE ALL SMASHED! WHAT HAPPENED?"

SUDDENLY, THE ROC LETS GO OF MARCO, AND HE FALLS INTO THE NEST.

MY EGGS ARE ALL DESTROYED! IT IS ALL YOUR FAULT!

I WOULDN'T SMASH YOUR EGGS. IN FACT, I NEED ONE OF THEM.

THE ROC FLAPS ITS MIGHTY WINGS ANGRILY. THE FORCE PUSHES MARCO BACK. MARCO HANGS ON WITH ALL HIS STRENGTH.

WOW! I'M BETWEEN A ROC AND A HARD PLACE ... HOW AM I GOING TO GET OUT OF THIS?

AFTER A WHILE, THE ROC CALMS DOWN. MARCO RELAXES A LITTLE. THE ROC PICK UPS BITS OF BROKEN SHELL AND DROPS THEM OVER THE SIDE.

MARCO DECIDES TO HELP.

TOGETHER, THEY TIP THE LARGEST PIECE OF SHELL OVER THE SIDE.

THE NEST IS NOW CLEAN. THE ROC TURNS TO MARCO AND SAYS ...

LET'S PLAY CHESS!

MARCO ... MARCO ... MARCO! MARCO! WAKE UP. ARE YOU ALL RIGHT?

IS IT REALLY YOU, TING LING? WHERE AM I? WHERE'S THE ROC? WHERE'S THE SPECIAL EGG?

SSSSHHHH! YOU MUST HAVE BEEN DREAMING, MARCO. THERE'S NO ROC HERE AND THERE'S NO EGG THAT I CAN SEE. LET'S GET BACK ON THE SHIP. WE WILL SAIL BACK TO THE GREAT KHAN.

WAIT, MARCO! LOOK! THERE'S THE EGG! YOU WERE USING IT AS A PILLOW!

BUT ... BUT ... I WAS PLAYING CHESS WITH THE ROC AND IT GAVE ME A SPECIAL EGG.

AND THERE IS THE EGG — HALF BURIED IN THE SAND.

The Roc's talons

AFRICA

Madagascar

THE LEGEND
OF THE ROC

Marco Polo claimed that he once saw a Roc — a bird so big that it could eat an elephant! Kublai Khan sent his men on a journey to Madagascar to find this bird.

The men brought back a feather that they said came from the Roc. It was very big — almost 40 times the size of a normal bird feather! The Khan believed their story. Today, experts think that the Khan's men probably brought back a leaf from the raffia palm!

There is proof that an enormous bird once lived on Madagascar, an island off the east coast of Africa. In 1850, a merchant found three eggs and some bones on the island. They were the largest bird eggs ever seen. Each egg was the size of 150 chicken eggs!

In 1866, scientists discovered a complete skeleton of a huge bird in Madagascar. It was ten feet tall and weighed about 1,000 pounds. This bird was like the ostrich — too heavy to fly!

A GIANT ROC, FULLY GROWN, SITS ON THE THRONE OF THE GREAT KHAN. IT STARES AT THEM CALMLY.

THERE ARE GASPS OF SURPRISE IN THE ROOM.

EVERYONE CLAPS WITH JOY. THE CURSE IS OVER.

THE ENTIRE COURT WATCHES AS MARCO AND THE GIANT ROC PLAY CHESS. THEY CHEER LOUDLY WHEN THE ROC NARROWLY WINS A TIE-BREAKING MATCH.

AFTER THE GAME, THE GIANT ROC FLIES AWAY.

WHAT A STORY!

YOUR STORIES WILL MAKE AN AMAZING BOOK.

I WILL CALL THE BOOK "THE DESCRIPTION OF THE WORLD."

ONE YEAR AFTER HIS CAPTURE, MARCO POLO IS RELEASED FROM PRISON.

HIS BOOK IS SOLD FAR AND WIDE. EVERYONE TALKS ABOUT HIS ADVENTURES. MARCO POLO BECOMES VERY FAMOUS.

Traders on the Silk Road

When the Mongols conquered China, Kublai Khan set up his capital city in northeast China.

The city was an important military and trading center. It was a natural stopping place for caravans traveling along the Silk Road, the great East-West trade route that stretched across Central Asia.

The city was the shape of a square and its walls were nearly 18 miles long. When Marco Polo visited the city, he was surprised by its magnificent palaces and treasures.

After the Mongol rule, the city became known as Peking, which means "northern city." Today it is called Beijing — the busy, modern capital city of the People's Republic of China.

DID MARCO MAKE IT ALL UP?

Marco Polo

When Marco Polo went back to Venice, he published a book about his travels called *The Description of the World.* Many people did not believe his stories. They called his book "A Million Lies."

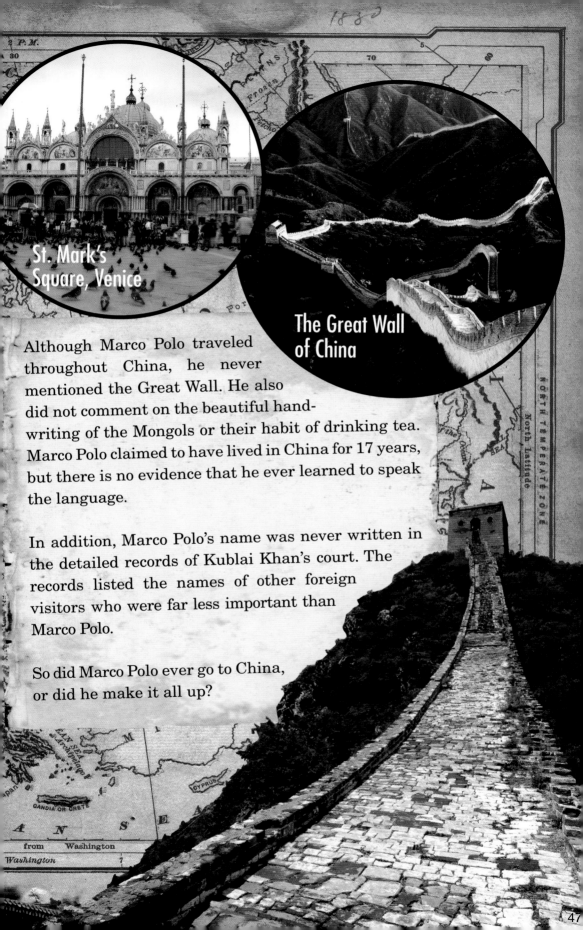

St. Mark's
Square, Venice

The Great Wall
of China

Although Marco Polo traveled throughout China, he never mentioned the Great Wall. He also did not comment on the beautiful handwriting of the Mongols or their habit of drinking tea. Marco Polo claimed to have lived in China for 17 years, but there is no evidence that he ever learned to speak the language.

In addition, Marco Polo's name was never written in the detailed records of Kublai Khan's court. The records listed the names of other foreign visitors who were far less important than Marco Polo.

So did Marco Polo ever go to China, or did he make it all up?

INDEX

A
Africa, 20, 37
America, 29
Asia, 4–5

B
Beijing, 5, 21, 45

C
Cambaluc, 4–5
Central Asia, 5, 45
China, 4–5, 7, 11, 21, 45, 47
Chinese junks, 29

E
Europe, 4–5, 21

G
Genoa, 13
Great Wall of China, 47

H
Hong Kong, 20

I
Italy, 4, 13

K
Kublai Khan, 4–5, 7, 11–12, 14–22, 34, 37–39, 41–42, 45, 47

M
Madagascar, 17, 19–20, 37
Marco Polo, 4–5, 7–8, 11–39, 42–47
Middle East, 5, 21
Mongols, 4–5, 21, 45, 47
Mozambique, 20

P
Persia, 4
Pisa, 13

R
Roc, 17–18, 22, 27–28, 30–37, 39, 41–43
Russia, 21
Rusti, 8, 32

S
Shanghai, 20
Silk Road, 45

T
Ting Ling, 15–16, 20, 23–25, 36, 38

V
Venice, 4–7, 13, 15, 18, 46